Excel Formula

By – Devbrat Rudra

1. SUM(range):

   - Use: Adds up all the numbers in a specified range.

   - Example: =SUM(A1:A10)

2. AVERAGE(range):

   - Use: Calculates the average of numbers in a specified range.

   - Example: =AVERAGE(B1:B5)

3. COUNT(range):

   - Use: Counts the number of cells that contain numbers in a specified range.

   - Example: =COUNT(C1:C100)

4. IF(logical_test, value_if_true, value_if_false):

   - Use: Performs a conditional test and returns one value if true and another if false.

   - Example: =IF(A1>10, "Yes", "No")

5. VLOOKUP(lookup_value, table_array, col_index_num, [range_lookup]):

   - Use: Searches for a value in the first column of a table and returns a value in the same row from another column.

   - Example: =VLOOKUP(A2, B1:D10, 3, FALSE)

6. HLOOKUP(lookup_value, table_array, row_index_num, [range_lookup]):

   - Use: Similar to VLOOKUP, but searches for a value in the first row of a table.

   - Example: =HLOOKUP(A2, B1:D10, 2, FALSE)

7. INDEX(range, row_num, column_num):

   - Use: Returns the value of a cell in a specified row and column of a range.

   - Example: =INDEX(A1:B10, 3, 2)

8. MATCH(lookup_value, lookup_array, [match_type]):

   - Use: Searches for a value in a range and returns its relative position.

   - Example: =MATCH(A2, C1:C100, 0)

9. IFERROR(value, value_if_error):

   - Use: Returns a specified value if a formula results in an error; otherwise, it returns the result of the formula.

   - Example: =IFERROR(A1/B1, "Error")

10. CONCATENATE(text1, text2, ...):

   - Use: Combines multiple text strings into one.

   - Example: =CONCATENATE(A1, " ", B1)

11. LEFT(text, num_chars):

   - Use: Returns a specified number of characters from the beginning of a text string.

   - Example: =LEFT(A1, 5)

12. RIGHT(text, num_chars):

- Use: Returns a specified number of characters from the end of a text string.

- Example: =RIGHT(A1, 3)

13. LEN(text):

- Use: Returns the number of characters in a text string.

- Example: =LEN(A1)

14. TRIM(text):

- Use: Removes leading and trailing spaces from a text string.

- Example: =TRIM(A1)

15. DATE(year, month, day):

- Use: Returns the serial number of a particular date.

- Example: =DATE(2023, 1, 1)

16. NOW():

- Use: Returns the current date and time.

- Example: =NOW()

17. RAND():

- Use: Returns a random decimal number between 0 and 1.

- Example: =RAND()

18. UPPER(text):

- Use: Converts text to uppercase.

- Example: =UPPER(A1)

19. LOWER(text):

   - Use: Converts text to lowercase.

   - Example: =LOWER(A1)

20. COUNTIF(range, criteria):

   - Use: Counts the number of cells in a range that meet a specific condition.

   - Example: =COUNTIF(A1:A100, ">50")

Certainly! Here are 30 more Excel formulas along with brief explanations of their uses:

21. COUNTA(range):

   - Use: Counts the number of non-empty cells in a specified range.

   - Example: =COUNTA(A1:A100)

22. SUMIF(range, criteria, [sum_range]):

   - Use: Adds up numbers in a range based on a given condition.

   - Example: =SUMIF(B1:B100, ">50", C1:C100)

23. AVERAGEIF(range, criteria, [average_range]):

   - Use: Calculates the average of numbers in a range based on a specified condition.

   - Example: =AVERAGEIF(A1:A10, "<>0")

24. IFNA(value, value_if_na):

   - Use: Returns a specified value if a formula results in a #N/A error.

- Example: =IFNA(VLOOKUP(A2, B1:D10, 3, FALSE), "Not Found")

25. SUMIFS(sum_range, criteria_range1, criteria1, [criteria_range2, criteria2], ...):

- Use: Adds up numbers based on multiple conditions.

- Example: =SUMIFS(C1:C100, A1:A100, "Category1", B1:B100, ">50")

26. AVERAGEIFS(average_range, criteria_range1, criteria1, [criteria_range2, criteria2], ...):

- Use: Calculates the average based on multiple conditions.

- Example: =AVERAGEIFS(D1:D100, A1:A100, "Category1", B1:B100, ">50")

27. INDEX-MATCH-MATCH:

- Use: Uses two MATCH functions to find the intersection of a row and column in a table.

- Example: =INDEX(B2:E5, MATCH("Product2", A2:A5, 0), MATCH("Week3", B1:E1, 0))

28. IFERROR(value, value_if_error):

- Use: Handles errors in a formula, returning a specified value if an error occurs.

- Example: =IFERROR(1/0, "Error: Division by zero")

29. TEXT(value, format_text):

- Use: Converts a value to text using a specified format.

- Example: =TEXT(NOW(), "yyyy-mm-dd hh:mm:ss")

30. NETWORKDAYS(start_date, end_date, [holidays]):

- Use: Calculates the number of whole workdays between two dates, excluding weekends and specified holidays.

  - Example: =NETWORKDAYS(A1, A2, B1:B10)

31. DATEDIF(start_date, end_date, unit):

   - Use: Calculates the difference between two dates in years, months, or days.

   - Example: =DATEDIF(A1, A2, "d")

32. SUBTOTAL(function_num, range1, [range2], ...):

   - Use: Performs a specified subtotal function (e.g., SUM, AVERAGE) on a range, ignoring other subtotals in the range.

   - Example: =SUBTOTAL(9, C1:C100)

33. ROUND(number, num_digits):

   - Use: Rounds a number to a specified number of digits.

   - Example: =ROUND(A1, 2)

34. ROUNDUP(number, num_digits):

   - Use: Rounds a number up, away from zero, to a specified number of digits.

   - Example: =ROUNDUP(A1, 0)

35. ROUNDDOWN(number, num_digits):

   - Use: Rounds a number down, towards zero, to a specified number of digits.

   - Example: =ROUNDDOWN(A1, 0)

36. SUMPRODUCT(array1, [array2], ...):

- Use: Multiplies corresponding components in the given arrays and returns the sum of those products.

   - Example: =SUMPRODUCT(A1:A10, B1:B10)

37. INDEX-MATCH with Multiple Criteria:

   - Use: Uses the INDEX and MATCH functions with multiple criteria to retrieve specific data from a table.

   - Example: =INDEX(D2:D100, MATCH(1, (A2:A100="Category1")*(B2:B100>50), 0))

38. TRANSPOSE(array):

   - Use: Transposes rows and columns in a given array.

   - Example: =TRANSPOSE(A1:B3)

39. LOOKUP(lookup_value, lookup_vector, result_vector):

   - Use: Searches for a value in a lookup vector and returns the corresponding value from the result vector.

   - Example: =LOOKUP(A2, B2:B10, C2:C10)

40. CHOOSE(index_num, value1, [value2], ...):

   - Use: Chooses a value from a list based on its position.

   - Example: =CHOOSE(A1, "Option1", "Option2", "Option3")

41. INDIRECT(ref_text, [a1]):

   - Use: Returns the value of a cell specified by a text string.

   - Example: =INDIRECT("A1")

42. MATCH with Wildcards:

   - Use: Uses wildcards in the MATCH function to find approximate matches.

   - Example: =MATCH("apple*", A1:A100, 0)

43. HYPERLINK(link_location, [friendly_name]):

   - Use: Creates a hyperlink in a cell.

   - Example: =HYPERLINK("https://www.example.com", "Visit Example")

44. IF(AND(logical1, logical2, ...), value_if_true, value_if_false):

   - Use: Performs a logical AND operation and returns a value if all conditions are true.

   - Example: =IF(AND(A1>10, B1<5), "Yes", "No")

45. IF(OR(logical1, logical2, ...), value_if_true, value_if_false):

   - Use: Performs a logical OR operation and returns a value if any condition is true.

   - Example: =IF(OR(A1>10, B1<5), "Yes", "No")

46. IF(ISNUMBER(value), value_if_true, value_if_false):

   - Use: Checks if a value is a number and returns different values based on the result.

   - Example: =IF(ISNUMBER(A1), "Numeric", "Not Numeric")

47. IF(ISBLANK(cell), value_if_true, value_if_false):

   - Use: Checks if a cell is blank and returns different values based on the result.

   - Example: =IF(ISBL

ANK(A1), "Blank", "Not Blank")

48. INDEX-MATCH with Dynamic Range:

- Use: Uses INDEX and MATCH with dynamic ranges that automatically adjust as new data is added.

- Example: =INDEX(OFFSET(A1,0,0,COUNTA(A:A),1), MATCH("Product2", OFFSET(A1,0,0,COUNTA(A:A),1), 0))

49. COUNTBLANK(range):

- Use: Counts the number of blank cells in a specified range.

- Example: =COUNTBLANK(A1:A100)

50. RANK.EQ(number, ref, [order]):

- Use: Returns the rank of a number in a list, with the option to specify ascending or descending order.

- Example: =RANK.EQ(B2, B1:B10, 1)

Certainly! Here are 25 more Excel formulas along with brief explanations of their uses:

51. OFFSET(reference, rows, cols, [height], [width]):

- Use: Returns a reference offset from a starting cell or range of cells.

- Example: =OFFSET(A1, 1, 2)

52. IF(ISTEXT(value), value_if_text, value_if_not_text):

- Use: Checks if a value is text and returns different values based on the result.

- Example: =IF(ISTEXT(A1), "Text", "Not Text")

53. IFERROR(value, value_if_error):

  - Use: Returns a specified value if a formula results in an error.

  - Example: =IFERROR(1/0, "Error: Division by zero")

54. CHOOSE(index_num, choice1, [choice2], ...):

  - Use: Returns a value from a list based on its position.

  - Example: =CHOOSE(A1, "Option 1", "Option 2", "Option 3")

55. SUMPRODUCT(array1, [array2], ...):

  - Use: Multiplies corresponding components in the given arrays and returns the sum of those products.

  - Example: =SUMPRODUCT(A1:A10, B1:B10)

56. CONCATENATEX(table, expression, [delimiter]):

  - Use: Concatenates the result of an expression for each row in a table, using an optional delimiter.

  - Example: =CONCATENATEX(Table1, [Column1], ", ")

57. TEXTJOIN(delimiter, ignore_empty, text1, [text2], ...):

  - Use: Joins together text from multiple ranges or strings with a specified delimiter.

  - Example: =TEXTJOIN(", ", TRUE, A1:A10)

58. IF(IFS(logical_test1, value_if_true1, [logical_test2, value_if_true2], ...), value_if_false):

- Use: Performs multiple logical tests and returns the value corresponding to the first true condition.

   - Example: =IF(IFS(A1>10, "High", A1>5, "Medium", TRUE, "Low"), "Yes", "No")

59. UNIQUE(range):

   - Use: Returns a list of unique values from a range.

   - Example: =UNIQUE(A1:A100)

60. FILTER(range, condition1, [condition2], ...):

   - Use: Returns an array that meets one or more specified conditions.

   - Example: =FILTER(A1:A100, B1:B100>50)

61. SEQUENCE(rows, [columns], [start], [step]):

   - Use: Generates a sequence of numbers in a specified range.

   - Example: =SEQUENCE(5, 1, 10, 2)

62. XLOOKUP(lookup_value, lookup_array, return_array, [if_not_found], [match_mode], [search_mode]):

   - Use: Searches a range or array, and returns an item corresponding to the first match found.

   - Example: =XLOOKUP(A2, B2:B10, C2:C10, "Not Found")

63. LET(name1, value1, [name2, value2], ..., expression):

   - Use: Defines variables and calculates a result in a single formula.

   - Example: =LET(x, 5, y, 10, x+y)

64. WEBSERVICE(url):

   - Use: Retrieves data from a web service and returns the result as a text string.

   - Example: =WEBSERVICE("https://api.example.com/data")

65. RANDARRAY(rows, [columns], [min], [max], [integer]):

   - Use: Generates an array of random numbers.

   - Example: =RANDARRAY(5, 3, 1, 100, TRUE)

66. SORT(range, [sort_index], [sort_order], [by_col]):

   - Use: Sorts a range of data.

   - Example: =SORT(A1:B10, 2, 1)

67. FORECAST.ETS(range, values, timeline):

   - Use: Predicts a future value based on existing values and a timeline.

   - Example: =FORECAST.ETS(A1:A10, B1:B10, C1:C10)

68. RRI(principal, n, [pmt], [fv], [type]):

   - Use: Calculates the relative rate of interest for an investment.

   - Example: =RRI(1000, 5, 50, 1200)

69. IRR(values, [guess]):

   - Use: Calculates the internal rate of return for a series of cash flows.

   - Example: =IRR(B1:B5, 0.1)

70. NPER(rate, pmt, pv, [fv], [type]):

- Use: Calculates the number of periods for an investment based on periodic payments and interest rate.

  - Example: =NPER(0.05, -200, 1000)

71. ISPMT(rate, per, nper, pv):

  - Use: Calculates the interest payment for a specific period in an investment.

  - Example: =ISPMT(0.05, 2, 5, 1000)

72. FV(rate, nper, pmt, [pv], [type]):

  - Use: Calculates the future value of an investment based on periodic payments and interest rate.

  - Example: =FV(0.05, 5, -200, -1000)

73. HARMEAN(number1, [number2], ...):

  - Use: Calculates the harmonic mean of a set of numbers.

  - Example: =HARMEAN(A1:A10)

74. GEOMEAN(number1, [number2], ...):

  - Use: Calculates the geometric mean of a set of numbers.

  - Example: =GEOMEAN(A1:A10)

75. WEIGHTED AVERAGE:

  - Use: Calculates the weighted average of a range of values.

  - Example: =SUMPRODUCT(A1:A5, B1:B5) / SUM(B1:B5)

Certainly! Here are 25 more Excel formulas along with brief explanations of their uses:

76. IRR (Internal Rate of Return):

- Use: Calculates the internal rate of return for a series of cash flows, where cash flows are irregular.

   - Example: =IRR(B1:B10)

77. MIRR (Modified Internal Rate of Return):

- Use: Calculates the modified internal rate of return for a series of cash flows, considering both reinvestment and financing rates.

   - Example: =MIRR(B1:B10, 0.1, 0.05)

78. DAYS360 (start_date, end_date, [method]):

- Use: Calculates the number of days between two dates based on a 360-day year.

   - Example: =DAYS360(A1, A2)

79. SUMPRODUCT with Multiple Criteria:

- Use: Adds up the product of corresponding components in arrays or ranges that meet multiple criteria.

   - Example: =SUMPRODUCT((A1:A10="Category1")*(B1:B10>50)*(C1:C10))

80. EOMONTH (start_date, months):

- Use: Returns the last day of the month, a specified number of months before or after the start date.

   - Example: =EOMONTH(A1, 3)

81. TODAY():

- Use: Returns the current date.

- Example: =TODAY()

82. MONTH (date):

- Use: Returns the month of a given date as a number (1-12).

- Example: =MONTH(A1)

83. YEAR (date):

- Use: Returns the year of a given date.

- Example: =YEAR(A1)

84. ROUNDUP (number, num_digits):

- Use: Rounds a number up, away from zero, to a specified number of digits.

- Example: =ROUNDUP(A1, 0)

85. ROUNDDOWN (number, num_digits):

- Use: Rounds a number down, towards zero, to a specified number of digits.

- Example: =ROUNDDOWN(A1, 0)

86. ROUND (number, num_digits):

- Use: Rounds a number to a specified number of digits.

- Example: =ROUND(A1, 2)

87. CEILING (number, significance):

- Use: Rounds a number up to the nearest multiple of significance.

- Example: =CEILING(A1, 5)

88. FLOOR (number, significance):

   - Use: Rounds a number down to the nearest multiple of significance.

   - Example: =FLOOR(A1, 5)

89. RANDBETWEEN (bottom, top):

   - Use: Returns a random integer between the specified bottom and top values.

   - Example: =RANDBETWEEN(1, 100)

90. INDEX-MATCH with Multiple Criteria and Multiple Results:

   - Use: Retrieves multiple results from a table based on multiple criteria using INDEX and MATCH.

   - Example: {=INDEX(C2:C10, MATCH(1, (A2:A10="Category1")*(B2:B10>50), 0))} (Enter as an array formula)

91. SUBTOTAL with Dynamic Range:

   - Use: Uses SUBTOTAL with dynamic ranges that automatically adjust as new data is added.

   - Example: =SUBTOTAL(9, OFFSET(A1, 0, 0, COUNTA(A:A), 1))

92. NORM.S.DIST (z, cumulative):

   - Use: Returns the standard normal distribution for a specified z-score.

   - Example: =NORM.S.DIST(A1, TRUE)

93. NORM.INV (probability):

   - Use: Returns the inverse of the standard normal distribution for a specified probability.

   - Example: =NORM.INV(A1)

94. IF(AND(OR(logical1, logical2), logical3), value_if_true, value_if_false):

   - Use: Performs nested logical AND and OR operations in an IF statement.

   - Example: =IF(AND(OR(A1>10, B1<5), C1=0), "Yes", "No")

95. INDEX-MATCH with Wildcards:

   - Use: Uses wildcards in the MATCH function for approximate matches.

   - Example: =INDEX(A2:A100, MATCH("app*", B2:B100, 0))

96. SUMIFS with OR Logic:

   - Use: Uses SUMIFS with OR logic to sum values based on multiple criteria.

   - Example: =SUMIFS(C1:C100, A1:A100, "Category1", B1:B100, {"High","Medium"})

97. IFERROR with VLOOKUP:

   - Use: Combines IFERROR and VLOOKUP to handle errors in a lookup formula.

   - Example: =IFERROR(VLOOKUP(A2, B1:D10, 3, FALSE), "Not Found")

98. INDEX-MATCH with Dynamic Array:

   - Use: Uses INDEX and MATCH with dynamic arrays to automatically adjust results as new data is added.

   - Example: =INDEX(A:A, MATCH("Product2", B:B, 0))

99. XLOOKUP with Wildcards:

   - Use: Utilizes wildcards in XLOOKUP for approximate matches.

   - Example: =XLOOKUP("app*", B2:B100, C2:C100, "Not Found")

100. ARRAY FORMULAS:

- Use: Perform calculations on arrays of data using functions that can handle multiple values at once.

- Example: {=SUM(A1:A10*B1:B10)} (Enter as an array formula)

Certainly! Here are 25 more Excel formulas along with brief explanations of their uses:

101. XIRR (External Rate of Return):

- Use: Calculates the internal rate of return for a series of cash flows with specified dates.

- Example: =XIRR(B1:B10, A1:A10, 0.1)

102. XMATCH (lookup_value, lookup_array, [if_not_found], [match_mode], [search_mode]):

- Use: Searches a range or array, and returns the relative position of an item.

- Example: =XMATCH(A2, B2:B10, "Not Found", 1, 0)

103. TEXT (value, format_text):

- Use: Converts a value to text using a specified format.

- Example: =TEXT(NOW(), "yyyy-mm-dd hh:mm:ss")

104. CONCAT (text1, [text2], ...):

- Use: Joins together multiple text strings.

- Example: =CONCAT(A1, " - ", B1)

105. FILTERXML (xml, xpath):

- Use: Extracts data from XML content using an XPath query.

- Example: =FILTERXML("<root><data>Value</data></root>", "//data")

106. WEIGHTED SUM:

- Use: Calculates the weighted sum of a range of values.

- Example: =SUMPRODUCT(A1:A5, B1:B5)

107. IF(ISTEXT(value), value_if_text, value_if_not_text):

- Use: Checks if a value is text and returns different values based on the result.

- Example: =IF(ISTEXT(A1), "Text", "Not Text")

108. SUMPRODUCT with Multiple Arrays:

- Use: Adds up the product of corresponding components in multiple arrays.

- Example: =SUMPRODUCT(A1:A5, B1:B5, C1:C5)

109. CHISQ.DIST.RT (x, degrees_freedom):

- Use: Returns the right-tailed probability of the chi-square distribution.

- Example: =CHISQ.DIST.RT(A1, 3)

110. HYPERLINK (link_location, [friendly_name]):

- Use: Creates a hyperlink in a cell.

- Example: =HYPERLINK("https://www.example.com", "Visit Example")

111. CUMIPMT (rate, nper, per, start_period, end_period, type):

- Use: Calculates the cumulative interest paid between two periods.

- Example: =CUMIPMT(0.05, 5, 2, 1, 5, 0)

112. CUMPRINC (rate, nper, per, start_period, end_period, type):

   - Use: Calculates the cumulative principal paid between two periods.

   - Example: =CUMPRINC(0.05, 5, 2, 1, 5, 0)

113. STDEV.P (number1, [number2], ...):

   - Use: Estimates the standard deviation based on a sample.

   - Example: =STDEV.P(A1:A10)

114. STDEV.S (number1, [number2], ...):

   - Use: Calculates the standard deviation based on the entire population.

   - Example: =STDEV.S(A1:A10)

115. SLOPE (known_y's, known_x's):

   - Use: Calculates the slope of the linear regression line through a given set of data points.

   - Example: =SLOPE(B1:B10, A1:A10)

116. INTERCEPT (known_y's, known_x's):

   - Use: Calculates the y-intercept of the linear regression line through a given set of data points.

   - Example: =INTERCEPT(B1:B10, A1:A10)

117. FORECAST (x, known_y's, known_x's):

   - Use: Predicts a y-value based on a linear regression model.

   - Example: =FORECAST(A11, B1:B10, A1:A10)

118. TEXT to Columns:

- Use: Splits text in a cell into multiple columns using a specified delimiter.

- Example: Select the cell, go to the "Data" tab, and choose "Text to Columns."

119. FREQUENCY (data_array, bins_array):

- Use: Calculates the frequency distribution of a set of data.

- Example: =FREQUENCY(A1:A100, B1:B5)

120. NORM.DIST (x, mean, standard_dev, [cumulative]):

- Use: Returns the normal distribution for a specified x-value, mean, and standard deviation.

- Example: =NORM.DIST(A1, B1, C1, TRUE)

121. SUMPRODUCT with SUMIFS:

- Use: Combines SUMPRODUCT with SUMIFS for more complex criteria.

- Example: =SUMPRODUCT(SUMIFS(A1:A5, B1:B5, "Category1"), C1:C5)

122. FORMULATEXT (cell_reference):

- Use: Returns a formula as text from a given cell reference.

- Example: =FORMULATEXT(A1)

123. RANK.AVG (number, ref, [order]):

- Use: Returns the rank of a number in a list, with the average rank for duplicate values.

- Example: =RANK.AVG(B2, B1:B10, 1)

124. RANK.EQ with Ties (number, ref, [order]):

- Use: Returns the rank of a number in a list, handling ties by assigning the same rank.

- Example: =RANK.EQ(B2, B1:B10, 1)

125. TREND (known_y's, [known_x's], [new_x's], [const]):

- Use: Predicts y-values based on the linear trend of a set of data.

- Example: =TREND(B1:B10, A1:A10, A11:A15)

Certainly! Here are 50 more Excel formulas along with brief explanations of their uses:

126. EFFECT (nominal_rate, npery):

- Use: Calculates the effective annual interest rate based on the nominal rate and compounding frequency per year.

- Example: =EFFECT(A1, B1)

127. NOMINAL (annual_rate, npery):

- Use: Converts the annual interest rate to the nominal rate given the number of compounding periods per year.

- Example: =NOMINAL(A1, B1)

128. IRR with Multiple Investments:

- Use: Calculates the internal rate of return for multiple investments with varying cash flows.

- Example: =IRR({-1000, 200, 200, 200, 200}, 0.1)

129. CUMPRODUCT with Criteria:

- Use: Multiplies corresponding components in arrays that meet specific criteria.

  - Example: =SUMPRODUCT((A1:A10>5)*(B1:B10<50)*C1:C10)

130. FORMULATEXT (cell_reference):

  - Use: Returns a formula as text from a given cell reference.

  - Example: =FORMULATEXT(A1)

131. CONCATENATEX (table, expression, [delimiter]):

  - Use: Concatenates the result of an expression for each row in a table, using an optional delimiter.

  - Example: =CONCATENATEX(Table1, [Column1], ", ")

132. TEXTJOIN with Array:

  - Use: Joins together text from multiple ranges or strings with a specified delimiter.

  - Example: =TEXTJOIN(", ", TRUE, A1:A10, B1:B10)

133. IFS with Multiple Conditions:

  - Use: Performs multiple logical tests and returns a value corresponding to the first true condition.

  - Example: =IFS(A1>10, "High", A1>5, "Medium", TRUE, "Low")

134. UNION with Arrays:

  - Use: Combines two or more arrays into a single array.

  - Example: =UNION(A1:A5, B1:B5)

135. SUBTOTAL with Dynamic Array:

   - Use: Uses SUBTOTAL with dynamic arrays that automatically adjust as new data is added.

   - Example: =SUBTOTAL(109, OFFSET(A1, 0, 0, COUNTA(A:A), 1))

136. SEQUENCE with Dynamic Array:

   - Use: Generates a sequence of numbers in a specified range.

   - Example: =SEQUENCE(COUNT(A1:A100), 1, 1, 1)

137. SLN (cost, salvage, life):

   - Use: Calculates the straight-line depreciation of an asset for one period.

   - Example: =SLN(A1, B1, C1)

138. SYD (cost, salvage, life, period):

   - Use: Calculates the sum-of-years-digits depreciation of an asset for a specified period.

   - Example: =SYD(A1, B1, C1, D1)

139. VDB (cost, salvage, life, start_period, end_period, [factor], [no_switch]):

   - Use: Calculates the depreciation of an asset for any period, including partial periods, using the double declining balance method.

   - Example: =VDB(A1, B1, C1, D1, E1, F1, G1)

140. MID (text, start_num, num_chars):

   - Use: Returns a specific number of characters from a text string, starting at the specified position.

   - Example: =MID(A1, 3, 5)

141. LEN (text):

   - Use: Returns the number of characters in a text string.

   - Example: =LEN(A1)

142. LOWER (text):

   - Use: Converts text to lowercase.

   - Example: =LOWER(A1)

143. UPPER (text):

   - Use: Converts text to uppercase.

   - Example: =UPPER(A1)

144. PROPER (text):

   - Use: Capitalizes the first letter of each word in a text string.

   - Example: =PROPER(A1)

145. SEARCH (find_text, within_text, [start_num]):

   - Use: Returns the starting position of one text string within another text string.

   - Example: =SEARCH("apple", A1)

146. SUBSTITUTE (text, old_text, new_text, [instance_num]):

   - Use: Replaces occurrences of a specified substring with another substring in a text string.

   - Example: =

SUBSTITUTE(A1, "red", "green")

147. TRIM (text):

- Use: Removes leading and trailing spaces from a text string and reduces multiple spaces between words to a single space.

- Example: =TRIM(A1)

148. VALUE (text):

- Use: Converts a text string that represents a number to a numerical value.

- Example: =VALUE(A1)

149. IFERROR with INDEX-MATCH:

- Use: Handles errors in an INDEX-MATCH formula.

- Example: =IFERROR(INDEX(B1:B10, MATCH(A1, A1:A10, 0)), "Not Found")

150. IFERROR with VLOOKUP:

- Use: Combines IFERROR and VLOOKUP to handle errors in a lookup formula.

- Example: =IFERROR(VLOOKUP(A1, B1:D10, 3, FALSE), "Not Found")

151. RANK.AVG with Multiple Criteria:

- Use: Returns the average rank of a number in a list, considering multiple criteria.

- Example: =RANK.AVG(B2, B1:B10, C1:C10, 1)

152. RANK.EQ with Multiple Criteria:

- Use: Returns the rank of a number in a list, considering multiple criteria.

- Example: =RANK.EQ(B2, B1:B10, C1:C10, 1)

153. XLOOKUP with Multiple Criteria:

   - Use: Searches a range or array, and returns an item corresponding to the first match found, considering multiple criteria.

   - Example: =XLOOKUP(1, (A1:A10="Category1")*(B1:B10>50), C1:C10)

154. INDEX-MATCH with Multiple Criteria and OR Logic:

   - Use: Retrieves a value based on multiple criteria using INDEX and MATCH with OR logic.

   - Example: {=INDEX(C2:C10, MATCH(1, (A2:A10="Category1")*((B2:B10>50)+(B2:B10<10)), 0))} (Enter as an array formula)

155. INDEX-MATCH with Multiple Criteria and Multiple Results:

   - Use: Retrieves multiple results from a table based on multiple criteria using INDEX and MATCH.

   - Example: {=INDEX(C2:C10, MATCH(1, (A2:A10="Category1")*(B2:B10>50), 0))} (Enter as an array formula)

156. XLOOKUP with Wildcards and Multiple Criteria:

   - Use: Utilizes wildcards in XLOOKUP for approximate matches and considers multiple criteria.

   - Example: =XLOOKUP("app*", (B2:B100="Category1")*(C2:C100>50), D2:D100, "Not Found")

157. SUMIFS with Dynamic Range and OR Logic:

   - Use: Uses SUMIFS with dynamic ranges that automatically adjust and OR logic for multiple criteria.

- Example: =SUMIFS(OFFSET(A1, 0, 0, COUNTA(A:A), 1), OFFSET(B1, 0, 0, COUNTA(B:B), 1), "Category1", OFFSET(C1, 0, 0, COUNTA(C:C), 1), {"High","Medium"})

158. INDEX-MATCH with Dynamic Array and Error Handling:

   - Use: Uses INDEX and MATCH with dynamic arrays and error handling.

   - Example: =IFERROR(INDEX(A:A, MATCH("Product2", B:B, 0)), "Not Found")

159. XLOOKUP with Dynamic Range and Wildcards:

   - Use: Utilizes XLOOKUP with dynamic ranges that automatically adjust and wildcards for approximate matches.

   - Example: =XLOOKUP("app*", OFFSET(B1, 0, 0, COUNTA(B:B), 1), OFFSET(C1, 0, 0, COUNTA(C:C), 1), "Not Found")

160. SUMPRODUCT with Dynamic Ranges and Criteria:

   - Use: Uses SUMPRODUCT with dynamic ranges and criteria.

   - Example: =SUMPRODUCT(OFFSET(A1, 0, 0, COUNTA(A:A), 1), OFFSET(B1, 0, 0, COUNTA(B:B), 1), (OFFSET(C1, 0, 0, COUNTA(C:C), 1)="Category1")*(OFFSET(D1, 0, 0, COUNTA(D:D), 1)>50))

161. INDEX-MATCH with Wildcards and Dynamic Array:

   - Use: Uses wildcards in the MATCH function for approximate matches with dynamic arrays.

   - Example: =INDEX(OFFSET(A1,0,0,COUNTA(A:A),1), MATCH("Product*", OFFSET(B1,0,0,COUNTA(B:B),1), 0))

162. SUMIFS with Multiple Criteria and Dynamic Range:

   - Use: Uses SUMIFS with dynamic ranges that automatically adjust and multiple criteria.

- Example: =SUMIFS(OFFSET(A1, 0, 0, COUNTA(A:A), 1), OFFSET(B1, 0, 0, COUNTA(B:B), 1), "Category1", OFFSET(C1, 0, 0, COUNTA(C:C), 1), ">"&D1)

163. INDEX-MATCH with Dynamic Range and Multiple Results:

   - Use: Uses INDEX and MATCH with dynamic ranges and retrieves multiple results.

   - Example: {=INDEX(OFFSET(C2, 0, 0, COUNTA(C:C), 1), MATCH(1, (OFFSET(A2, 0, 0, COUNTA(A:A), 1)="Category1")*(OFFSET(B2, 0, 0, COUNTA(B:B), 1)>50), 0))} (Enter as an array formula)

164. SUMPRODUCT with INDEX-MATCH and Dynamic Range:

   - Use: Combines SUMPRODUCT with INDEX-MATCH and dynamic ranges.

   - Example: =SUMPRODUCT(INDEX(OFFSET(A1, 0, 0, COUNTA(A:A), 1), MATCH("Product2", OFFSET(B1, 0, 0, COUNTA(B:B), 1), 0)), OFFSET(C1, 0, 0, COUNTA(C:C), 1))

165. INDEX-MATCH with Dynamic Array and Partial Match:

   - Use: Uses INDEX and MATCH with dynamic arrays for a partial match.

   - Example: =INDEX(OFFSET(A1, 0, 0, COUNTA(A:A), 1), MATCH("*Partial*", OFFSET(B1, 0, 0, COUNTA(B:B), 1), 0))

166. **COUNTIFS (criteria_range1, criteria1, [criteria_range2, criteria2], ...):**

   - **Use:** Counts the number of cells that meet multiple criteria.

   - **Example:** `=COUNTIFS(A1:A100, "Category1", B1:B100, ">50")`

167. **SUMPRODUCT with INDEX-MATCH:**

   - **Use:** Combines SUMPRODUCT with INDEX-MATCH for more flexible calculations.

- **Example:** `=SUMPRODUCT(INDEX(C1:C10, MATCH(A2, B1:B10, 0)), D1:D10)`

168. **CELL (info_type, [reference]):**

   - **Use:** Returns information about the formatting, location, or contents of a cell.

   - **Example:** `=CELL("address", A1)`

169. **FORMULA (reference):**

   - **Use:** Returns the formula in a specified cell.

   - **Example:** `=FORMULA(A1)`

170. **VBA Macros:**

   - **Use:** Executes custom VBA (Visual Basic for Applications) code to automate tasks.

   - **Example:** VBA code is typically entered and executed in the VBA editor.

171. **PMT (rate, nper, pv, [fv], [type]):**

   - **Use:** Calculates the periodic payment for an annuity.

   - **Example:** `=PMT(0.05, 5, -1000)`

172. **FV (rate, nper, pmt, [pv], [type]):**

   - **Use:** Calculates the future value of an investment.

   - **Example:** `=FV(0.05, 5, -200, -1000)`

173. **PV (rate, nper, pmt, [fv], [type]):**

   - **Use:** Calculates the present value of an investment.

- **Example:** `=PV(0.05, 5, -200, 0, 0)`

174. **HLOOKUP with Dynamic Column Index:**

   - **Use:** Performs an HLOOKUP with a dynamically changing column index.

   - **Example:** `=HLOOKUP("Week3", B1:E1, MATCH("Product2", A2:A5, 0), FALSE)`

175. **INDEX-MATCH with Multiple Results and Dynamic Range:**

   - **Use:** Retrieves multiple results from a table based on multiple criteria using INDEX and MATCH, with a dynamic range.

   - **Example:** `{=INDEX(C2:C100, MATCH(1, (A2:A100="Category1")*(B2:B100>50), 0))}` (Enter as an array formula)

176. **NORM.INV with Probability:**

   - **Use:** Returns the value for a standard normal distribution based on a specified probability.

   - **Example:** `=NORM.INV(A1)`

177. **SKEW.P (number1, [number2], ...):**

   - **Use:** Calculates the skewness of a distribution based on a sample.

   - **Example:** `=SKEW.P(A1:A10)`

178. **KURT.P (number1, [number2], ...):**

   - **Use:** Calculates the kurtosis of a distribution based on a sample.

   - **Example:** `=KURT.P(A1:A10)`

179. **TIME (hour, minute, second):**

- **Use:** Creates a time value from given hour, minute, and second components.

  - **Example:** `=TIME(12, 30, 0)`

180. **DATEVALUE (date_text):**

   - **Use:** Converts a date in the form of text to a serial number.

   - **Example:** `=DATEVALUE("2023-01-01")`

181. **TIMEVALUE (time_text):**

   - **Use:** Converts a time in the form of text to a serial number.

   - **Example:** `=TIMEVALUE("12:30:00 PM")`

182. **MINIFS (range, criteria_range1, criteria1, [criteria_range2, criteria2], ...):**

   - **Use:** Finds the minimum value in a range based on multiple criteria.

   - **Example:** `=MINIFS(A1:A100, B1:B100, "Category1", C1:C100, ">50")`

183. **MAXIFS (range, criteria_range1, criteria1, [criteria_range2, criteria2], ...):**

   - **Use:** Finds the maximum value in a range based on multiple criteria.

   - **Example:** `=MAXIFS(A1:A100, B1:B100, "Category1", C1:C100, ">50")`

184. **MID (text, start_num, num_chars):**

   - **Use:** Returns a specific number of characters from a text string, starting at the specified position.

   - **Example:** `=MID(A1, 2, 3)`

185. **SEARCH (find_text, within_text, [start_num]):**

   - **Use:** Returns the starting position of one text string within another, case-sensitive.

   - **Example:** `=SEARCH("apple", A1)`

186. **ROUND to Nearest Multiple:**

   - **Use:** Rounds a number to the nearest specified multiple.

   - **Example:** `=ROUND(A1, 5)`

187. **ROUND with Significant Digits:**

   - **Use:** Rounds a number to a specified number of significant digits.

   - **Example:** `=ROUND(A1, 3)`

188. **LOOKUP with Approximate Match:**

   - **Use:** Searches for a value in a range and returns the corresponding value with an approximate match.

   - **Example:** `=LOOKUP(85, A1:A10, B1:B10)`

189. **UNION with Named Ranges:**

   - **Use:** Combines multiple named ranges into one.

   - **Example:** `=UNION("Range1", "Range2")`

190. **INTERSECT with Named Ranges:**

   - **Use:** Returns the intersection of two or more named ranges.

   - **Example:** `=INTERSECT("Range1", "Range2")`

191. **FORMULATEXT with Dynamic References:**

   - **Use:** Returns the formula as text from a cell with dynamic references.

   - **Example:** `=FORMULATEXT(INDIRECT("A1"))`

192. **POWER (number, power):**

   - **Use:** Raises a number to a specified power.

   - **Example:** `=POWER(A1, 2)`

193. **UNION with Dynamic Ranges:**

   - **Use:** Combines multiple ranges into one using dynamic references.

   - **Example:** `=UNION(A1:B10, INDIRECT("D1:E10"))`

194. **INTERSECT with Dynamic Ranges:**

   - **Use:** Returns the intersection of two or more ranges using dynamic references.

   - **Example:** `=INTERSECT(A1:B10, INDIRECT("C1:D10"))`

195. **PERCENTILE.INC (array, k):**

   - **Use:** Returns the kth percentile of values in a dataset, inclusive.

   - **Example:** `=PERCENTILE.INC(A1:A100, 0.25)`

196. **PERCENTILE.EXC (array, k):**

   - **Use:** Returns the kth percentile of values in a dataset, exclusive.

   - **Example:** `=PERCENTILE.EXC(A1:A100, 0.25)`

197. **QUARTILE.INC (array, quart):**

- **Use:** Returns the quartile of a dataset, inclusive.

- **Example:** `=QUARTILE.INC(A1:A100, 3)`

198. **QUARTILE.EXC (array, quart):**

   - **Use:** Returns the quartile of a dataset, exclusive.

   - **Example:** `=QUARTILE.EXC(A1:A100, 3)`

199. **HLOOKUP with Dynamic Column Index and Range:**

   - **Use:** Performs an HLOOKUP with a dynamically changing column index and range.

   - **Example:** `=HLOOKUP("Week" & ROW(A1), $B$1:$E$1, 2, FALSE)`

200. **TODAY with Custom Format:**

   - **Use:** Returns the current date with a custom format.

   - **Example:** `=TEXT(TODAY(), "dd-mmm-yyyy")`

201. **SUMIFS with OR and AND Logic:**

   - **Use:** Uses SUMIFS with both OR and AND logic for complex criteria.

   - **Example:** `=SUMIFS(C1:C100, A1:A100, "Category1", B1:B100, ">"&D1, B1:B100, "<"&E1)`

202. **IFS with Nested OR Conditions:**

   - **Use:** Uses nested IFS functions to handle multiple OR conditions.

   - **Example:** `=IFS(OR(A1>10, B1<5), "High", AND(A1>5, A1<=10), "Medium", TRUE, "Low")`

203. **TRANSPOSE with Dynamic Range:**

- **Use:** Transposes a range of cells dynamically as data changes.

- **Example:** `=TRANSPOSE(OFFSET(A1,0,0,COUNTA(A:A),1))`

204. **SORT with Dynamic Range and Criteria:**

    - **Use:** Sorts a range based on specified criteria and adjusts dynamically.

    - **Example:** `=SORT(OFFSET(A1,0,0,COUNTA(A:A),3), 2, -1)`

205. **CHOOSE with Dynamic Index:**

    - **Use:** Returns a value from a list based on a dynamically changing index.

    - **Example:** `=CHOOSE(MATCH("Product2", A1:A5, 0), B1, B2, B3, B4, B5)`

206. **HYPERLINK with Dynamic URL:**

    - **Use:** Creates a hyperlink with a dynamically changing URL.

    - **Example:** `=HYPERLINK("https://example.com/" & A1, "Link")`

207. **SUMPRODUCT with SUMIFS and Dynamic Range:**

    - **Use:** Combines SUMPRODUCT with SUMIFS and dynamic ranges for complex calculations.

    - **Example:** `=SUMPRODUCT(SUMIFS(C1:C100, A1:A100, "Category1"), D1:D100)`

208. **NORM.S.INV (probability):**

    - **Use:** Returns the inverse of the standard normal distribution for a specified probability.

    - **Example:** `=NORM.S.INV(A1)`

209. **DATE with Dynamic Components:**

- **Use:** Creates a date using dynamically changing components.

- **Example:** `=DATE(YEAR(TODAY()), MONTH(TODAY()), DAY(TODAY())+7)`

210. **SUMIFS with Dynamic Criteria Range:**

- **Use:** Uses SUMIFS with a dynamically changing criteria range.

- **Example:** `=SUMIFS(OFFSET(A1,0,0,COUNTA(A:A),1), OFFSET(B1,0,0,COUNTA(B:B),1), "High")`

www.ingramcontent.com/pod-product-compliance
Lightning Source LLC
LaVergne TN
LVHW081807050326
832903LV00027B/2134